GARDEN

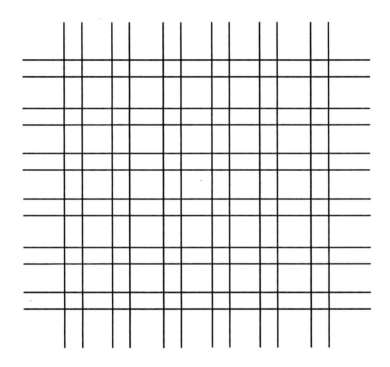

GardenMonty Reid

CHAUDIERE BOOKS MMXIV

for Frances Margaret Reid

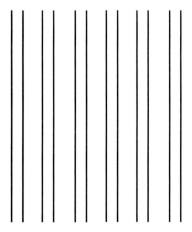

Garden (sept unit)

What is missing for most gardeners to make them feel like artists is a sufficiently harebrained plan....

Robert Harbison

1. September

All the stems
are hollow.

It's how the dead
breathe

there
in the anonymous ground

waiting for us
to go away.

2. October

The last under-ripe
Brussels sprouts

have been picked.

And eaten
again.

3. November

The first snow
arrives.

The imaginary
is never as cold

as the real
thing.

4. December

I have woken up
with blank spots
in my vision.

It could be serious

or it could be
the imaginary words

or the even more
beautiful ones.

5. January

It's too late.

The year
has always started
a long time ago

and your former
and your current loves
did too.

6. February

What you want to see
isn't visible.

What you want to see
isn't you.

Therefore, you
it seems to be

you are
and isn't.

7. March

Declension
stalks the snow cover.

It wonders how many people it is
how many mouths.

I was hungry
and you fed me.

And clean
ed up after.

8. April

Ah, new feet.

And the footprints
that still

aren't theirs.

9. *May*

In the paradoxical garden
only the status grow.

Confusion
of form, of number.

Color suctioned out of the ground
and suspended in the air's discourse

is no threat to anything.

10. *June*

The petals whisper
all our names.

Wait.

I mean the petals whisper
all my names.

I mean

all my name.

The petals I mean
don't do anything but whisper.

11. July

You broke the pod open
and can't close it again.

No, not the i-pod.

That's the difference.

You can close the i-pod again
and you will still be inside.

12. August

The old black walnut stump in the corner of the garden
nurses its lichen, its beetles, its ants.

Someone cut the tree down
long before I was here.

The subjects of interest are long gone.

I don't know who.
Just someone.

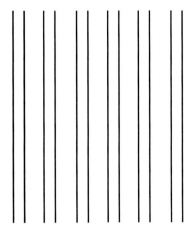

Garden (oct unit)

There at the centre of the boundless garden
The boundaries are still in place

Inger Christensen

1. *October*

They are thinking about what it means to be human
again.

They have thought that to be human means to substitute.

For instance, every time 'other' appears, use 'garden' instead.

A prosthetization of the animate or the human that not only
makes it difficult to rigorously distinguish the human from its
inanimate garden.

There is, of course, no substitute for the garden.

2. *November*

They are thinking about what it means to be human.

They have found that this is more of a problem for thinking
than for living.

Does the garden suffer, now, in the first serious cold
of the year?

Do they realize it is now impossible to say 'garden' without
reproducing some whiff of the 'other'?

Maybe they should substitute something else.

3. December

The garden is pure illusion now.

What is memory is another garden.

Both of them.

4. January

I am lost in this profusion of gardens.
It is the only way.

The gardener puts his hand on the immediate.
To be the touch of the cabbage.

To be the touch of the small potatoes.

Each consciousness pursues the death of the garden.
To be this touch, and its disappearance.

5. *February*

I am awake at midnight.

A gentle snow is falling where I remember the garden.
A gentle snow is falling on the replacement of the garden

and elsewhere.

6. *March*

Je est un garden.
Its resistance is so small.

Labour is arbitrary but work is not.

When I speak of outcome, I am expressing an inevitable uncertainty.
When I speak of uniqueness, I am also expressing the location of the garden.

Which is right out there, working.

7. April

Being functional
is what makes possible a transformation of functions.

Food is the resistance of the garden.
Squash has no value as an idea.

Beans make you fart.
There is no garden of the garden.

8. May

I dug up the lawn and hauled in 10 yards of dirt
and shoveled it over the back yard
and my hands hurt.

The garden is not a conceptual life.
My back hurts.

Tomatoes sprout in the undecided light
but sprout, thank goodness
anyway.

There is more compassion in 10 yards of dirt
than a spoonful of idea.

9. *June*

The garden comes before me.
With all of its history.

But I am, nonetheless, in the garden
trying to distinguish the carrots from the weeds.

10. *July*

I used to think that if one inserted 'the good Lord'
every time you came across the word 'language'
you'd get a sense of the complementary relation
between poetry and tv evangelists.

And I thought if you substituted 'money'
for 'language' the commodification
of poetry by its theorists
would be explicit.

Now, I did not used to think
I would think less in the garden
just think better.

11. *August*

Already the sunflowers have grown so tall
they can look over the fence
and they do.

My neighbors are in their yard
suntanning naked.

I can't see them, but the sunflowers tell me.

12. *September*

Tomatoes knocked over by the rain.

And still, they were thinking as if that is what it meant
to be human.

Acids shine in the wet dirt as what shone in the mind.

That meant, in the end
that you have think of something else or it will not grow.

Garden (nov unit)

The book was a sort of protection because it had a better plot. If any can be spared from the garden..

Lyn Hejinian

1. *November*

Presence is the ghost of snow.

The dog of frost chews its bone.

On an old black walnut stump in the corner of the garden
a pumpkin waits with its carved-up face
and its one sweet tooth.

It spent one night on fire
and is now abandoned by the light.

But even on the first day of November, with no one to see
it's still laughing.

2. *December*

The inhabited is a confined space.

How can we be sure that the body she addresses
even belongs to her?

The garden is not global.
It is the specifics of what will grow here

which is not eggplant
I guess.

3. January

Who, then, among the multiple animals
could be said to live here?

Even now, in the deepest part of the year
I can smell the space of her.

None of them, in this space
could be said to live only here.

4. February

Yes

useless valentines
are better
than all others

sd Jack Spicer
if I remember correctly.

Useless pumpkins too.

5. March

Again, I come to the garden
and find no one

except the pumpkin
still weighted with snow and its face caved in.

It has nothing to say
yet its laughter continues

in whatever I still think I might be.

6. April

Sprouts started in old milk cartons
begin their privileged life in the south window.

And still, they plot their escape.

They lean at the light, because they think there may be a place
where they are necessary.

They examine the milk cartons again.
More carefully this time.

7. May.

Ah, Jack, I mean Jack the pumpkin
that's the last of you.

Just an orange smear even the crows ignore.
Maybe you didn't even know you were in the garden.

The mouth and eyes collapse
the face is first to go.

And the iridescent beetles and ants are hard at work
filling up on what you said, what you think you saw.

8. June

The systems theorists prefer the system
to be people-free

so it's good to have a friend, here in the garden.
Language has gotten restless, it's true

but that doesn't mean it wants you to stop
pulling at its edges.

The dirt doesn't need a memory
but it has one anyway.

9. *July*

Eating the small yellow pear tomatoes.

Yes
they are shaped like teardrops.

10. *August*

How, among all this flourish.

Just how.

11. *September*

The faces of the dead want nothing but recognition.

Whatever they say, language
isn't alive.

It doesn't matter.
The dead aren't alive either.

12. *October*

The pumpkins
are ready for their faces.

Will we make them look serious this year?
As if they actually believed their own rhetoric?

Maybe they just can't live in this world anymore.

Still, they scare the crap out of the little kids.

Garden (dec unit)

And I have gone walking slowly
in his garden of necessity

Phyllis Webb

1. December

There are those who want the world to be observable
because it is unobservable

what the world looks like when we're not there
is there, not as symptom

but as there, tilted towards the imagined
gift, as the kiss

in December moonlight.

2. January

Is the garden new?
Does it hollow out the snow, which needs to be hollowed
out by something.

Like the shadows that hollow out the cave, or the systems
that teach themselves
whatever it was that was human.

Among the many elsewheres
December moonlight frays the edges of what that was.

3. *February*

An astringent moon sits in the limpid air.
It wants to come back

as something other than image
but the forms you have to fill out are endless.

Pale bitter day.
I have been trying to hear the sound of the garden.

Its broken silences, its gravitational
pull

and there is nothing
but dried-out moonlight all afternoon.

4. *March*

Does the self-regulating system just sound like
another version of market economics
to you?

Does the system that speaks only to itself
not sound like an endlessly proliferating bureaucracy
to you?

You need to work in the garden
before you can decide how to green the offices
before you are the living wall.

5. April

Thaw

has a boundary
and an unmarked space excluded by the boundary.

It is not art, but everything
splits the real world into a real world and an imaginary world.

A shovel, for instance.

6. May

I am digging in the garden with my non-transcendental
shovel.

Over the years, my hands have smoothed the short wooden handle.
The blade is worn down too.

I am wearing an old sweatshirt with Tyrrell Museum written on it.
I am wearing an old pair of Wrangler jeans.
I am wearing heavy Kodiak socks.
I am wearing lace-up Sorel workbooks.
I am wearing a sweat-stained ballcap from the Ottawa Folk Festival.
I am wearing a pair of ragged canvas gloves from Home Depot
I am wearing Stanfields underwear, I hope.

Yes, that's me.

7. June

If our apprehension of the world cannot be contained
by thinking – at least not by thinking as philosophy has traditionally
conceived it – then the last thing we should do
is try to think it again.

It's not my garden.
I just worked there.

8. July

The garden isn't there to see it.
Although it now swarms with the observed.

The tangles of peas climb into the sunlight
then they fall over.

There is too much to eat
so I am giving away what I can't use.

Trust me, the peas
you can't see taste the best.

9. August

My imagination is such a cliché.
Yours too, probably.

Can you imagine the assistant deputy minister
of the garden standing there in a suit

and all the squash blossoms interrupting
their journey beyond the garden for a moment

to look back at him, or her.

Me neither.

10. September

The edge conditions have become a little gangly.

The garden is lit up
with just about everything

even with all those little lights off in the distance
the trimmed-back stars.

11. *October*

Response is where responsibility begins.

Already I have forgotten what the garden
looks like.

Organic matter burns in this light.
Burns like evidence.

12. *November*

If you talk about the garden long enough
it begins to talk about you.

It says you're just a plot for the flora and fauna

It says you're not a pure form, not pure being
Not pure anything.

It knows you have no plan.
And it knows then that it has talked too much.

Garden (jan unit)

It wasn't born in a garden, but it certainly
was born in a history.

Donna J. Haraway

1. *January*

How long have you been wanting the garden
not to exist?

At the deep end of winter all the animals sleep
except you.

I thought we wanted this together.
I thought we were innocent.

No, that's not true – I never thought we were innocent.
I just thought the garden might relieve us

of our need to be innocent.
And it doesn't.

2. *February*

How long have you been wanting the garden
not to exist?

You may as well tell me.

Maybe we can denounce the present world together.
Tomatoes from the store taste like cardboard.

Maybe the snow
won't melt.

3. *March*

How long have you been wanting the garden
not to exist?

Forever, forever.

Even now that you know
90% of the genetic material in the human body
is not mine

and neither is the rest?

2. *April*

The shovel is my companion species.
The hoe is my helper brain.
The fork is my gmo.
The boot is my choreography.

The dirt is my prosthesis.
What sort of order should we cling to?
April is my shower.
Yes, April is my shower.

5. *May*

The rake prints where I tamped the dirt down
on the rows of seeds

look like stitches.

Something has to hold the garden together.
After the rake has been removed

and I don't miss it anymore.

6. *June*

So many green fins in the garden

what swims underneath?

Between the air and under the air.

You'll notice this isn't about description.

The world doesn't end there.

Look down, unless it scares you.

7. July

Just let them have some.
They will have some anyway.

Let them assemble, without the insecticidal soup.
They will assemble anyway.

Oh the chitin is striated and iridescent
isn't it?

When they are all here
ask them.

8.August

The attachment site
is beautiful

because something attaches.

There is no ready-made paradise
just waiting to be named.

Here, everything is already named.
It just wants to eat.

9. *September*

How long have you been wanting the garden
not to exist?

Are all gardens copies of other gardens?
Is there a plan for eden that you could refer to?

Of course not.
The original breath never happened.

But you can still feel the warm
air against your ear before you can hear it.

Like a baby's whisper
that doesn't know yet what it will say.

10. *October*

Now that there's nothing left to guard
three crows have come to protect the garden.

They have been here before
They are the crows of subtraction.

Do they know where everything is buried?

They better.

11. *November*

Do you think it's that easy
to now let's become someone else?

There is a long list of things you can never be.
What I want to be is always another thing.

Do you think it's easy to do the work of the garden.

With all the seeds to bury.
And the dirt that turns over but never stays turned over.

And the ghosts that divide
but never stay divided.

12. *December*

I awake well past midnight with a strange light
in the room.

Light with something missing in it.
Some little string of code.

Snow in the garden.

You have been returned, with pieces missing.

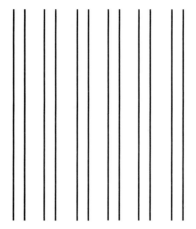

Garden (feb unit)

and all my gardens grew backwards
and all the roots were finally square

Gwendolyn MacEwan

1. *February*

The garden has never trusted what we do.
The great faith-healers have come and gone
collecting their remedies.

And still, the recurring limbs ache their phantom ache.

But the garden always has the same problem.
It has never been human.

Every now and the then, the turnips
think of transcendence.

Sometimes they think of the apparat, the tools
that are not their own. But it's rare.

2. *March*

My mother loved the hymn that begins
'I come to the garden alone'.

She got rid of the lawn, and planted the entire front yard
in flowers. The back yard, however, was all vegetables.

No olive trees, unlike the Garden of Gethsemane.

No roses to collect the dew.
No betrayal. Nothing to heal.

3. April

There is much of paradise but very little of the garden.

In the poems of Wallace Stevens, for instance.

When the garden exceeds its enclosure it is erotic.
I mean when the dirt comes from somewhere else it is erotic.
When the friction of rain in New Haven
comes from somewhere else.

Another New Englander, Robert Frost, had more of the garden
and unloved walls. He kept running into Stevens down in Miami
where they both went in the winter, and where
they vigorously disagreed.

4. May

I would be afraid to enter the knot garden
even for maintenance purposes.

The tight boxwood of its edges smells sweet
or like cat urine.

Light sits on the sage like the dust of heaven.

The thyme and balms are clipped and trimmed
as angels.

Every sweater I wore has unraveled.
Every noose has let me fall.

5. June

The garden always tries to keep something
out.

Ghosts, for instance.
They're out.

Once they were sleep.
Now they're the ghosts of sleep.

They're out too.

6. July

There's only so much self to go around.
This is why the system of the garden must appear
to keep things out.

Because such appearance is the only way to keep things in.
Take the Hanging Gardens of Babylon, which
were designed to keep the Queen in.

Nonetheless, they were destroyed by an earthquake
and never rebuilt.

7. August

The scarlet runner beans
climb over the fence.

The complacencies in the middle of the garden
are declarative.

You can grab them and try to hang on to them
but they're gone.

8. September

The Isles of the Blest
are protected.

They have security
by the daughters of the west.

By the many nymphets
and their surveillance.

There are times
when I just want to fuck them all.

9. *October*

Whatever is unavailable to the world
remains available to the bugs.

The garden has been unable to reduce the bugs
and has agreed to feed them instead.

Which is what all systems do when they discover
they cannot reduce the complexity of the world.

They feed the bugs. The lovely bugs
that circulate in the flesh.

The lovely bugs that somehow winter over.

10. *November*

What didn't grow this year:

Parsnips – and I planted them twice.
Brussels sprouts – planted too late.
Eggplant – nothing at all.

Rhubarb – transplanted two clumps
and they didn't get well rooted.

Lettuce – strangely enough.
The squash overwhelmed it.

When this is gone
I will tell you this again.

11. December

I am contemplating the Ryoan-ji Garden in Kyoto.
I can only see 14 of the 15 famous rocks.

It is early morning and the furrows of white pebbles
are raked into their pretend eroticism.

Raked, and the rake is gone.
Plum blossoms above the wall.

What remains within this poem.

12. January

My garden is there to be eaten.

Eaten.
Not Eden.

All writing is about something.

Garden (march unit)

The other garden
Flourishes.
Under absolute neglect.

Robert Kroetsch

1. *March*

If I think, must the turnip also be conceptual?

I think the heft of things.

Here, to emphasize their natural nuttiness and complexity,
they're gently glazed with butter, then sprinkled with
garlicky toasted breadcrumbs and abundant poppy seeds.

2.*April*

Whatever is conceptual must be of use.
Like a chef's notes.

Even though the potato is fundamentally utilitarian.
Its eyes see in the dark.
Or maybe its eyes just see you, in the dark.

If you can't find goose or duck fat, use an equal amount of
butter instead.

3. *May*

I had a garden in the badlands. In the silt of old rivers.
We fed the soil, therefore the cucumbers are conceptual.

The cucumber creates an object, not a mediation.
Among the old rivers, time is not a mediation.

So-called Persian cukes seem especially beautiful against a
background of exotic purple jasmine rice.

4. *June*

Where is the desire of the radish?

Down there at the apical tip, in the dendrite arbors
that knit the dirt into memory.

See, there is an answer to everything.

Puree all ingredients in a blender until very smooth.

5. July

Broccoli is an exception.
Broccoli is the idea exhausted in its execution.

It wishes to be embraced by freedom and yet
look how the beads cluster together tightly
susceptible to mildew.

Cooking cruciferous vegetables without boiling them, as in
this recipe, seems to make them more fragrant and heady—
just the way the robust Romans like their food.

6. August

She is kneeling In the garden.
On knee pads that she got from Lee Valley Tools.

Instruction is everywhere. The garden is full
of golden leaves and the jobs that still remain for you to do.

No. All the jobs still remain for you to do.

In addition to the fried parsnip the executive chef at
Ashford Castle often adorns this soup with a poached
carved apple.

7. September

Therefore the corn is conceptual.
Therefore.

Corn is a paradoxical commodity.
Does it listen?

Since there's no way to stop it from listening therefore
you go on talking.

The corn pudding can also be made in individual serving
sizes. Simply bake in small ramekins.

8. October

The eggplant is a work of failure.

Something was saved. No, not the body.
Who would want to save that?

The eggplant does not love you but is compelled
towards you nonetheless.

Eggplant can be grilled using a gas grill. Preheat all burners
on high, covered, 10 minutes, then reduce heat to medium.

9. *November*

The pumpkin keeps grinning
after halloween's over

and I don't know why.

In the garden, a woman keeps grinning at the pumpkin
that will never have a face.

It's a light and flavorful soufflé consisting mostly of egg
whites, a great source of high-quality protein.

10. *December*

I think, therefore asperge is conceptual.

Asperge can be conceived of.
Open or closed.

Why keep fighting that old battle.

Asparagus can be cooked (without butter and lemon) 1
day ahead. Drain asparagus, then immediately plunge into
a bowl of ice and cold water to stop cooking. Drain again
and chill in a sealed plastic bag lined with dampened paper
towels.

11. *January*

I think, therefore the arugula is always
incomplete. This is the bitterness of anything conceptual.

Arugula is the properly melancholic contemporary entity.
Even under the gro-light in the basement.

Programmed never to go off.

Wild arugula is dark green with spiky leaves. It has a more
intense flavor than that of regular arugula. You'll find wild
arugula at farmers' markets and at some supermarkets.

12. *February*

I think, therefore the beet
may be the only thing left that is not conceptual.

Take off the nightskin.
The beet is the difference between negative and positive
space.

The beets are nestled in a pool of almond butter and
crowned with a glorious Gorgonzola bombolone.

Garden (april unit)

One day gardens will come to get you.

Joshua Clover and Juliana Spahr

1. April

The garden is an enclosure
but a failed enclosure.

It was never intended to be perfect.
Theoretical rigor always fails but

the sex was great.

In the garden
who is less important than where.

Of course.

2. May

Clouds oppose the wind.

Is that what they do?
Is that why they break apart?

There is no language
only words.

It is not quite a clear day.
Then it is.

3. *June*

The birds start early.
You can tell they plan to sing all day.

There are times when that would make me happy
but not now.

I'm too sleep-deprived to want to communicate.
In all my dreams I am dying.

A noose tightens, the plane flips over in the clouds
above Commonwealth Stadium just before the Grey Cup,
assassins with night-vision goggles hunt for someone in the dark
of the National Arts Centre, somehow the room begins to flood
and there's no way out.

Whatever.
As long as the birds shut the fuck up.

4. *July*

How old will I be this month?
Must be a typo.

God, the young are so breathless
and so full of words

none of which they trust.

Repeat that again. None of which they trust.
The only way to resist is slow down.

5. *August*

Love finds something
there and changes it.

Try to imagine something
free of you.

The garden changes.
You are not imagining it.

6. *September*

The little pear tomatoes fall on the ground.
Every morning I pick a bowl full and bring them in to you.

There are too many to eat.

The little pear tomatoes communicate nothing.
They look like tears, or expensive little microphones

but they record nothing.

Say whatever you need to say.

7. October

You are my commensal
my companion species

You are so naked there is nothing left but your body.

The fingers of the right hand wander, as she claims.
The fingers of the left, also.

They drag along that opposable thumb.

8. November

I would dig a hole
if there wasn't one already.

I would rake a leaf
if there wasn't one already.

I would say your name
if there wasn't one already.

9. *December*

Nothing left in the garden except some chard
and squash in the freezer.

Nothing left of the light except some darkness.
Nothing left except what it isn't.

And you are still hungry.
You are still revealed.

10. *January*

The shovel hangs in the shed
with its rust.

Perhaps it already knows too much.

Perhaps its guilt overwhelmed it.

We should cut it down and give it a proper burial.

Or we could just leave it there
as a warning to the rest of them.

11. *February*

The secret for enlivening regular plans is violation.

I don't want you to get the wrong idea
about the garden.

It's 640 square feet in the back of a large city lot
in the east end of Ottawa.

Where the weeds come up regularly.
Perhaps that is the plan. Maybe

I'm not the only one with this problem.

12. *March*

Ah paradise, it's full of bones.

The sky presses down.

Go put on your coat, one long arm
and then the other

as if you were removing yourself
from all of the uncovered space

and may not return.

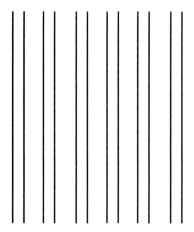

Garden (may unit)

Remembering or forgetting is doing
gardener's work....

Marc Augé

1. *May*

Once you're in the garden, how do you get out?
After you've nibbled the lettuce.

The endless regression
of voices

makes you smaller.

No, one pill does that.

2. *June*

Gardeners don't care about your identity.
The shovel has its mysteries but you have to dig
anyway.

Did the phenomena depend on us?
And we were always unreliable?

Now all that's left is objects.
You could get stuck, like Peter Rabbit
in the watering can.

You will never know what kind of person it should be

until you are out of it.

3. *July*

Flicker of luciferin in the peripheries.

Fireflies in the marshes near the abandoned army base.

A beacon out on Duck Island for the river boats.

Stars fall through the air
or their light does

then escapes.

4. *August*

Ok, perhaps beauty has failed us
but the carrots haven't.

Here on Beacon Hill, not far from the foundations of the old lighthouse
the dirt is mostly idealistic silt.

It has time to recall how it drifted through the old sea, how it spalled
from the old continent, how its edges have been
tumbled smooth.

Truth is the runoff of practice.
It always needs some compost and peat dug into it.

The carrots are ready to come out of the ground.
Just wipe them on your pantleg before you try them.

Beauty is tooth, tooth beauty.

5. September

What is solid in the world
makes its reparations.

Heft of Yukon Gold.

Was the Jenny Lind melon
named after her voice or her bosom?

There is much
to ask forgiveness for.

6. October

In the garden it is impossible to ignore
the imperfections that give rise to many interesting physical phenomena
as the theory of solids recommends

weak interactions

squash walks

the susurrus of cucumbers.

7. November

The garden never works as meaning.
It is density and texture
and what happens when you eat.

The garden needs to be un-haunted
all those tensions of all those not-quite-there things
that might somehow be a self.

The resist of cell walls
and then their disappearance.

8. December

My daughter took her first solid food
On Dec 15.

It was a puree of sweet potatoes in breast milk.
I wish I could say the potatoes came from the garden.

Why can't I say that?
Is there anything to prevent me from saying that?

Could there be enough truth to poetry
enough truth to overlook all the flaws?

In that case, the breast milk came from the garden too.

9. *January*

All that`s left now is the float.

A dream garden suspended above the site
like the tremulous conditions of a life.

Kept in place by some twitchy current.

Like the one that makes you want to spend money
when you're broke

Especially that one.

10. *February*

It's still there, the sort-of
visible image of a garden

like something you should see in 3-d
but you don`t have the glasses or the necessary belief.

The garden is supposed to be more solid than that
you remind yourself.

Are we out of turnips?

11. *March*

But we desire it too.

The garden will not do what it's told.

12. *April*

Love finds something
there and changes it.

The ordinary shimmers with it
small things that begin to fly
in the wands of unseasonably warm sunlight

that get what they can out of the ordinary
before it disappears.

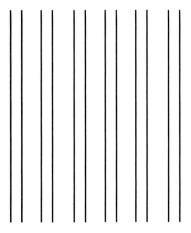

Garden (june unit)

And less alone there, a garden is, in short,
an open link bent on forming more, ever
outward, a line between humans and other
species, falling open....

Cole Swenson

1. *June*

I made a scarecrow out of an old sweatshirt
with Tyrrell Museum written on it.

And some old Wrangler jeans.
And Kodiak socks.
Some lace-up Sorel workbooks.
A sweat-stained ballcap from the Ottawa Folk Festival.
A pair of ragged canvas gloves from Home Depot.
And Stanfields underwear.

Yes, it's me, I think
every time I enter the garden again.

2. *July*

I prefer gnomic to cryptic,

because garden gnomes are supposed to
work happily in the garden at night.

And we could use some help.

I'd like a gnome molded out of resin, as they are these days
in a miniature form of Mackenzie King.

With a fedora and not the pointy hat
gnomes usually come with.

He could help with the vegetables
unlike the last time around.

3. August

Gardeners don't care about your positionality.
They just care about what you do.

So far, the scarecrow has kept nothing out.

4. September

The garden gnomes, which I stole from the embassy
are laughing.

The inukshuks, which I stole from the river
are laughing.

The little donkey, which I stole from Kingsmere,
is laughing.

All of the statuary, in all of the gardens
is laughing.

Because.

5. October

Because they have all been stolen

except for the emperor of gnomes, who remains
in a Cairo madhouse, according to.

They don't have to worry about their originary selves
and they don't have to worry about ownership.

They just work here.

6. November

There is a home-made sundial in the yard
and it's true, its shadow follows me around all morning

or the light follows me around
and that useless thing just gets in the way.

7. December

For Christmas Sarah gave me a lightweight gardener's belt
from Lee Valley I suspect.

It's made of non-degradeable synthetic fabric with big
polished grommets and green trim.

It has one large pocket for seeds
and three smaller mesh pockets for shears and string

and whatever else a gardener might need to carry
to the place where the codes are scattered.

I tried it on right away. I strode around the house
like I was planning something.

After I took all my clothes off.
And it fit.

8. January

The first day of the new year
Is dull and grey. Fog hangs on the black branches.

Narratives in tatters.
Narratives in taters, more like it.

9. February

The gnomes are sleeping underground.
In the luvisol, in saline or calcareous material
mixed by earthworms.

Have they murdered their daughters?
No, no, the daughters are running the show.

Wouldn't you, after a party like that?

10. *March*

The toad lived under a plank beside the garbage can.
He rarely came out, and when he did he hated the gnomes
and their political correctness.

He would pass slowly over the garden
and note, with some jaundice, the major changes.

There used to be goddesses, the anonymous
starlets of broken noses but goddesses nonetheless.
And now there's gnomes, the décor of garden bureaucracy.

The gnomes, he said, have endless paper
but no memory.

Nonetheless, neither the toad or the gnomes
have been able to abandon the garden.

11. *April*

Ah, the cruelest month
and it keeps coming back.

It substitutes a series of degraded words
for the formal languages.

Instead of those abstracted gardens
and their strap-on romances.

It has radishes, a lot
of radishes.

12. *May*

I waited til May
to try the new gardener's belt.

In the field, I mean.

Just the belt and some garden boots.

Spring moonlight, and the garden gnomes
nowhere in sight.

So you'll just have to take this word for it.

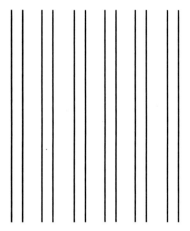

Garden (july unit)

I wanted to dig.

Michael Pollan

1. *July*

What will prolong this?
Because it wants to be prolonged.

One of those lazy summer evenings
where even a fine spray from the hose
feels like it could provoke redemptive violence.

Hasn't the garden taught you
that an interesting life always has something to hide.

The peas have overwhelmed their trellises.
They need the water.

2. *August*

What will prolong this?

Not because it wants to be prolonged.
But because the impersonal loop, the drifts of things
have never felt so intimate.

Some things stop.
And some, like the squash, which you have to hack off
just past the bud

don't know when.

3. September

What would be normal.
To be back to.

The beefsteak tomatoes are large and irregular.
Ribbed, multi-hued, punctured here and there by birds
crows maybe, and patrolled by ants.

When one of them falls
it is as if something has happened.

But maybe nothing
has.

4. October

Every time I walk into the garden
it feels like something has just happened

or that it was just starting
and I interrupted it.

There is the lurch of dream
along the thinned out rows.

I bring what I need in the toolbelt.

And a shovel.

5. *November*

Sooner or later
you feel alive.

And the only way you can stay alive
is to run like hell.

Both of you.
All of you.

The pumpkins stare at you
unable to move.

6. *December*

The raw bones of the wind are all that's left of it.

It blew all night and pushed the snow
into corners

Why would anyone bother to note that the garden
is a contested site

since all sites are contested
and all lives are made of the raw and unfashionable bones.

7. January

Ah, I am ready to transplant the moonlight.

Standing at the kitchen window
4am, and my daughter not quite asleep again
and the whole stars not quite asleep either.

The stillness has nothing to do with me.
And I have also gotten
tired of myself.

I live in a house that is not heated by all that light.

8. February

The fat ghosts.

That's all I can say.

The fat ghosts
are better than the thin ghosts.

9. *March*

The garden wolves don't show up.

Maybe because the ghosts keep them away
but there's no way of knowing that for sure.

The garden wolves now have a wilderness
somewhere

maybe as an art project in downtown Toronto.
No wonder.

10. *April*

There is an idea in the hollow of the garden.
Is just a theory the garden generates on the other side
of the garden.

All ideas are the same idea.
There is always another one that explains it better.

How then will one explain another garden?

11. *May*

It has no ambition to say.
It cannot speak for the original.
I t cannot speak even for last year's version.

The little dishes of radishes have appeared.
They swivel in the pulp of the garden.

Lettuce is running a surveillance operation.
Carrots slip their little probes out of the trenches.
And none of this has been approved.

It cannot speak because then we'd know where it came from.

12. *June*

As if we care.

The tendrils reach up into another part
of your life with a certain tension.

They swim towards the upper canopy of the garden
and its hair of light.

They have to fill you as if they were not your body
any more.

Garden (august unit)

There is nothing in a garden's structure that
will guarantee a story is read, let alone read
correctly, however insistent are its verbal
prompts.

John Dixon Hunt

1. *August*

To fill
the unfull

to complicate the music
to sip the tongue

to distract the bird of winds
to ignite the fireflies

to do this
is a bit of everything

that I have saved
and now let go.

2. *September*

Well, isn't that dramatic.

The big moon hangs there
like it was open-pollinated.

And all those heirloom seeds
don't you have to count them?

3. October

The birds hang upside down to clean out the sunflower seeds.
The squirrels fall off the scaffolding.
The rain barrel is full again, now that we don't need it.
The leaf attractor is working flat-out.

In the desert we have built a wall.
You can buy everything you need at Home Depot.
On the other side of the wall is paradise.
Not on this side either.

4. November

Fog on the tongue. As close
as it can get.

Balm rubbed into the skin

that burns
anyway.

5. December

Relax, you can't stop it now.

It's almost dawn, and the moon is outside your window.

Nothing grows there, in its plenitude.
In the heaven and earth machine.
In the fetish of its light.

Yet.

6. January

The lotus eaters and the rest of the bureaucrats
have their ambitions, their need to represent
all human concerns
                                        they will say
the garden survives in its names.

They will say we need the longest possible form
of the census, and still will miss a few potatoes

that overwinter in the dirt and show up unexpectedly
stubbornly green.

7. February

The old gardener's kiss could not separate the lips
of

or from

the lips of action.

In this reclaimed zone, after
the writing has passed.

In the zone of permanent exchange
where someone was made of warmth.

Not necessarily me.

8. March

Nonetheless, a warmth slowly returns.
And that's all it takes.

The simplest
the simplessed
and the simple-est

words
warm up first.

9. April

The schoolgirls think that because they have discovered
that all values are culturated, it ends there.

Signifiers can't heal them.
They think the progress of gardening will come about when.

But time passes beyond the last line
and illumination or freedom or grief
get stolen

or can be stolen again
and the first line can begin

or begins.

10. May

The apparat of voices grows, like everything else.
The more it claims to be radical the more desk-bound it gets.
The more it claims to disrupt the more it depends.

All the entities from elsewhere proliferate and still
the environment is never simpler than the place
it has been transformed into

and its loneliness.

11. *June*

I have dug up a fat black cutworm.
I blame it for the death of the cherry tomato plant
severed just above ground level.

It lies curled on the dirt like some version of an ear.
It has no voice, although it has paired black dots on its body
which may have a function.

It may turn into a grey moth upon which the birds would feed.

When I have called up all the tiny happinesses
I have turned into some version of a mouth.

12. *July*

Give us the garden.

Save us from paradise.

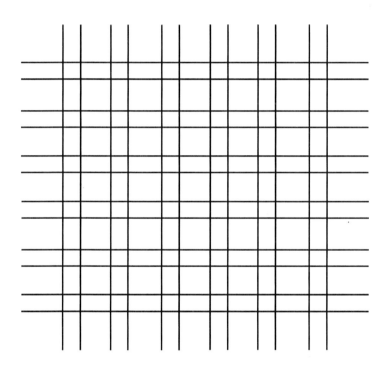

Biography

Monty Reid is a Canadian poet living in Ottawa. His most recent collection is *The Luskville Reductions* (Brick, 2008). His previous Chaudiere Books title, *Disappointment Island* was published in 2007. Recent chapbooks include *Site Conditions* (Apt 9), *Contributors' Notes* (Gaspereau) and *Moan Coach* (above/ground) along with Garden units from a variety of small presses. A three-time nominee for the Governor General's Award for Poetry, his work has won the Stephan G. Stephansson Award for Poetry three times, the Archibald Lampman Award for Poetry in 2007, and was shortlisted for the City of Ottawa Book Award. Much of Garden appeared as Facebook posts in 2012 and his current long work, *Intelligence,* appeared on Twitter throughout 2013. Other online work can be found at *Dusie, elimae, Drain, ottawater, Truck, experiment-o* and elsewhere. Recent print work can be seen in *The Peter F Yacht Club, The Malahat Review, Grain, Prairie Fire* and other magazines. He plays guitar and mandolin with the band Call Me Katie.

Acknowledgments

Real gardeners are considerably better-organized than I am. Planting times, weather and soil notes, frost dates, composting reminders and harvesting lists usually get recorded by diligent gardeners. I always forget. Instead, I get more interested in recording the decay of a post-Halloween jack-o-lantern or the chatter of the beetles. Similarly this book, which had its beginnings as a simple garden daybook, quickly moved off into more speculative plantings, none of which should be blamed on those who helped out along the way.

George Bowering's *My Darling Nellie Grey* was an early inspiration. Various other books, from writers such as Robert Harbison, Cole Swenson, Inger Christensen, Michael Pollan and Robert Kroetsch, were great companions. Much of *Garden* appeared as Facebook postings throughout 2012, and it was there that Argentine artist Andrea Bula encountered them. Her enthusiastic response, and translation into Spanish of many of the poems, led to a series of *Garden*-based paintings. She was unable to complete the project due to eye difficulties – one of her early sketches graces the cover. Christine McNair and rob mclennan, co-conspirators at Chaudiere Books, supported the project since its inception and I'm pleased to be part of the rejuvenated press. In addition, I am indebted to Lee Valley Tools and Ritchie's Seed and Feed for advice and bits of equipment. And to Sarah and Frances, my partners in the garden, my deepest thanks.

In addition to Facebook, these poems have appeared in various journals and as chapbooks. June unit first appeared in e-ratio. July unit appeared as a chapbook from obvious epiphanies press. Sept unit appeared as a chapbook from above/ground press. Oct unit appeared as a chapbook from LaurelReed Books. Nov unit appeared as a chapbook from Sidereal Press. Dec unit appeared as a chapbook from Corrupt Press. Jan unit appeared as a chapbook from red ceilings press. Feb unit appeared as a chapbook from grey borders press. Other poems have appeared in *Dusie* and *Event*. Thank you to the editors.

Colophon

This book was typeset in Jim Rimmer's Albertan Pro by Christine McNair and printed at Marquis Printing. Albertan was originally cut in 1982 as a metal typeface for handsetting limited edition books at Jim's Pie Tree Press. The digital version of Albertan was re-worked in 2012 by Canada Type designers as Albertan Pro.

Albertan transforms the traditional roman model by infusing many transitional traits without sacrificing the integrity of the calligraphic influence or the functionality of the overall setting. Twenty percent Albertan Pro family's sales are donated to the Canada Type Scholarship Fund, supporting higher typography education in Canada.

WWW.CHAUDIEREBOOKS.COM

Reid, Monty, 1952-
[Poems. Selections]
    Garden / Monty Reid.

Poems.
Some poems were previously published in limited edition
    chapbooks.
ISBN 978-1-928107-01-9 (PBK.)